About the Author

James Matthewson is a writer, author and political commentator from the north east of England. James grew up in the town of Alnwick, Northumberland. Aged twenty, he received a diagnosis of Asperger's Syndrome and began reflecting upon the challenges of growing up on the Autistic spectrum without a diagnosis. He began to highlight his experiences through poetry and the collection 'Wonderboy' was born. As the former spokesman to the Chair of the Labour Party and a commentator on UK politics, he regularly writes for publications including *The Times* and makes appearances on broadcast media. James now lives in rural Northumberland with his wife Lisa-Marie.

Wonderboy

James Matthewson

Wonderboy

(signature)
(MAMES).

Olympia Publishers
London

www.olympiapublishers.com
OLYMPIA PAPERBACK EDITION

Copyright © James Matthewson 2022

The right of James Matthewson to be identified as author of this work has been asserted in accordance with sections 77 and 78 of the Copyright, Designs and Patents Act 1988.

All Rights Reserved

No reproduction, copy or transmission of this publication may be made without written permission.
No paragraph of this publication may be reproduced, copied or transmitted save with the written permission of the publisher, or in accordance with the provisions of the Copyright Act 1956 (as amended).

Any person who commits any unauthorised act in relation to this publication may be liable to criminal prosecution and civil claims for damage.

A CIP catalogue record for this title is available from the British Library.

ISBN: 978-1-80074-579-7

First Published in 2022

**Olympia Publishers
Tallis House
2 Tallis Street
London
EC4Y 0AB**
Printed in Great Britain

Dedication

"I dedicate this book to my mother, Teresa Cairns, who passed away in March 2020. Without her, none of this would be possible."

Acknowledgements

I would like to thank the following people and organisations for their support of this book and its author; Lisa-Marie Kelly, Lesley Henderson, The Toby Henderson Trust, Annie Edgar, Professor Tony Attwood, Andy Payne and all of my supportive donors, friends and colleagues

Foreword

When I was at primary school, my mum was called in one day, possibly for the first time; or at least for the first time I could remember. There had been an incident. I cannot recall how I felt about it, but I do recall that being able to see my mum during the laboriously long school day would have been a welcome change from the drudgery of 'normality'.

Normality was not a concept I could identify with. It was something I longed for and wanted to be a part of, but I could not. During my limited experience of school so far, I had already worked out that I was not naturally likeable, I did not have the necessary football card trading knowledge to be cool nor did I have the skills of communication that seemed to come so effortlessly to many other kids.

As I sat in the school reception, I watched mum's car pull up outside and I felt immediately less anxious and more at ease with myself. This was my mum; she would sort out this big misunderstanding and make these foolish educators realise the error of their ways.

As Mum pushed open the door into the school (notably lacking in security during those carefree days of the late 1990s), I stood up and she gestured for me to sit and I obeyed, resuming the position I had been occupying for the last forty-six minutes. Whilst she signed in, she exchanged friendly words with the friendly lady who worked at the reception and always smelled of school dinners. Mum took a seat on a row of chairs opposite me and made brief and reassuring eye contact as the headteacher (let's call her Mrs S) came into view around the corner, her heels clicking loudly as she strutted down a shiny and clinical looking corridor. I remember that corridor looking like the inside of one of the film sets from Star Wars, but the reality of a state school in the North East of England resembling anything from a fictional sci-fi movie franchise from the 1970s leads me to conclude this is probably an embellishment added by my six-year-old brain.

Mrs S smiled and welcomed Mum; "Hello Teresa, thanks for coming in." A fact that was entirely lost on me at the time, but I now note with hindsight and just a pinch of embarrassment, just how unusual it must have been for a primary school headteacher to be in such regular contact with a parent that such a friendly, informal relationship was formed.

That is an essential feature of this story, but perhaps not a glowing endorsement of my behaviour.

"Happy to pop in and chat again." Mum smiled, "What's happened now?" She glanced from Mrs S's politely smiling face to my wide-eyed one and back again. I hate when grown-ups do this, how are you supposed to know at whom the question is directed?

I took it upon myself to assume control of the situation to save us all some precious time; "Nothing," I roared in outrage. Mum flashed an apologetic smile and

Mrs S returned a patient and understanding one as she gestured us toward an open door down the corridor that I had now internally nicknamed 'The Death star'. We took our places in this now well-rehearsed performance sitting at opposite sides of Mrs S' desk. Mum was offered coffee and tea, I was offered nothing (yet another example of the ongoing oppression and injustice facing children across the globe).

"Let's get straight to it," Mrs S said in her very serious voice. "James had been in class this morning with 'Mrs C' and there was an incident and James was sent straight to me," she pursed her lips as she added, "as has become the norm.". It was not unusual for teachers to use these very serious voices, it worked on some kids, but I wasn't one to fall for that sort of strategy.

"Okay, what happened?" Mum asked, now ignoring my presence entirely.

"According to Mrs C he swore at her and would not stop answering back. It was so disruptive she felt she had no option but to remove him from the class."

I could feel the anger bubbling up inside me, it started in my ankles and would rise through my knees and into my stomach. If I could contain it there, I might be able to remain calm, but the sheer cheek of it, the arrogance and the lies were too much. I was going to blow my lid. "That's not true. It's not true at all!" I screeched.

Mrs S was prepared, she'd seen this coming; "Why don't you tell me and your mum what happened then James? So that we can try to understand this."

Finally, I thought they would never ask, this was my chance to reveal the earth-shattering truth that I had no doubt would turn this experienced educator's world upside down. I took a deep breath and filled my young lungs with the breath I required to split the very atoms of the Northumberland County Council School System.

"Mrs C is a monster. I won't stand by while she abuses children and gets away with it." This got the reaction I had half-expected. Both Mum and Mrs S' mouths were agape. Part of me sensed that I had escalated things beyond a level of my understanding, but it was too late to turn back, the truth must come out. "She told Gemma, in my class, that if she didn't sit still, she would be in big trouble. Gemma then said; whatever, or something like that, and that's when it happened".

Mrs S was now writing in a notebook, God knows why. Mrs S looked up her face filled with anticipation "What happened James?".

I was careful to say the next bit as clearly as possible; I had been rehearsing it in my head for the past hour; "Mrs C called Gemma a stupid girl."

I waited for the inevitable outrage and the immediate action that would be taken to no doubt remove Mrs C from her position and ban her from the teaching profession forever more. Instead, there was a sigh of relief and a slight hint of frustration in my mum's voice; "And why did you get involved in this?"

"Because it's not right. You can't just say things like that to another person, especially not a child. So, I told her that and she then said the same to me. I told her she was stupid and was a stupid teacher. Everyone started laughing and she kicked me out."

Mrs S looked at my mum wearily and said, "This has

been the second incident of this type already this term. Last week, James called Mr A an idiot."

Mum asked me; "Why did you do that?"

The answer was obvious. Surely, they weren't going to take issue with this as well. "Mr A asked if anybody knew who the first man on the moon was. I put my hand up and he asked me for the answer, and I told him. He said I was wrong, and I called him an idiot because he didn't know the real answer."

Mrs S turned to Mum and gently added; "James said that his grandad was the first man on the moon, not Neil Armstrong."

Mum sighed. Taking one of grandad's stories as literal fact had caused trouble before, in fact this was very similar to the 'crocodile shoe' incident that left me with a grazed knee. "I believe James has difficulty in dealing with grey areas. He has a very clear idea in his mind of what is right and what is wrong. What is fact and what is not. He has a fascination in the world around him and watches everything very closely, but when it comes to his relationships with other pupils and teachers these misunderstandings are causing problems." Mum did not look very happy. I knew she had her suspicions; there was no escaping it, but perhaps now she was starting to realise that maybe her son wasn't as 'normal' as she might have hoped.

Mrs S was not the only teacher who would try to make my time within the mainstream school manageable. Over the next eleven years I would pass through a system that was not designed for me. I would feel useless, frustrated, angry and irritated. I would attend seven different schools and even be home educated for a period. I would face arguments, fights, suspensions, and expulsions and all the time without knowing what made me different.

Thankfully, with the constant support of an incredibly determined mother and later, a very patient step-father, I was able to scrape through and escape academia aged seventeen. And while similar challenges arose in my working life as a young adult, I never experienced an environment that seemed quite so inhospitable for somebody whose brain processed information in a different way. With encouragement from my mother, I was twenty years old when I was finally diagnosed with Asperger's Syndrome.

This book brings together a collection of poems and writings highlighting the experience of growing up with Asperger's and a large part of it deals directly with the impossibilities of navigating an education system that was designed to fit a very narrow mould.

I would like to dedicate this book to my mum, without whom, I would not be capable of communicating these experiences. I did not begin to collect and collate these disparate pieces of writing until after her death at the start of the world-wide Coronavirus Pandemic in 2020.

Secondly, I would like to dedicate this book to all the parents of Autistic children across the spectrum who are raising their own 'Wonderboy' or 'Wondergirl'. It is through your love, commitment, and dedication that stories like this one are possible. Lastly, I would also like to dedicate this book to those children and young people who are struggling to fit in or feel normal.

There will come a time when you realise just how incredible you are, and you will thank yourself and those who supported you for keeping you moving forward. One day, you will look back and see just how phenomenal your journey has been.

Asphalt Ghost

Trapped between worlds. Floating on the fringes. He haunts the corridors and toilets. Hidden in plain sight. Cloaked by selective invisibility. Wearing solitude like a chain mail vest. The warming light of day reveals him, only when scorn and jeer descend. He is present when alone, but painfully transparent in the deafening noise of playground crowds. Layers of screams and inside jokes roll over him like sea fret. If words are thrown, he solidifies, looking pale and feeling burnt. The sudden glare of attention stings flesh and flushes face. Headphones block out moments, fingers fuss in chewed up sleeves. If you look, which you will not, you'll see him, a shade of silent rage, an asphalt ghost.

Alone

Here is where thoughts come to race, the overheated
mind steaming like a blacksmiths bucket.
Spectral conversations haunt my neural pathways,
crossing wires as they go.
The silence rings in my ear drums, as protocol dictates
an evaluation of each faux pas in a
cringing analysis of interaction. Filling in my own
footprints I submit to forensic overthought and find a
natural comfort in
compulsion.

Wonderboy

Wonderboy in trouble.
He can't work out what burst his bubble, but he knows
his recent actions led to more dissatisfaction.
His peers, so called, were entertained but those adults,
whose praise he craved were angry at his rants and raves
and he now awaits the price he'll pay.

Wonderboy's in danger
He hears the mumbling of strangers.
It's all too loud, it's got him fuming.
The click and clack of teacher's shoes
Through shiny corridors behind him
There's a hurricane of words inside him.
Only she can calm the storm and right these wrongs he
has braved alone.

Wonderboy is saved.
The path for his escape is paved.
The door swings wide and fate reveals his sidekick's
shining sword and shield.
But the climate of his stomach shifts as he sees her face,
she's really miffed.
Surely she'd be on his side, as certain as the moon and
tide.
But as her head begins to shake, he's realised too late,

that wondrous wonderboy has made a grave mistake.

Wonderboy betrayed.
He had not foreseen this clever play.
To side with foe and wipe away, the love professed on normal days.
In the car returning home, her words were laced with angry tones.
She explained through tears the joy he'd robbed and how she'd had to leave her job.

Wonderboy reborn

He spent the night upstairs alone and though his thoughts were quite forlorn, he began to face what he had done.
He remembered how he'd been at school and his willingness to break the rules. He'd tried in vain to cause no pain, but her words repeated and replayed.

Stepping out into the night, he reached out for the hallway light and creaked downstairs on aching steps, to finish his important quest.
Head in hands she sat in peace and raised her head when in he sneaked.
Before he could even interrupt, his throat choked tight, and eyes filled up. Into her arms he fell at last, apologetic about the past.
I just want to be normal; I want to be liked, he cried, and he cried, and he cried and he cried.
'You'll always be different, and you may get annoyed, but I'll love you forever, my sweet Wonderboy.'

Algebra

This is your last warning, she screams, veins pulsating
in a beetroot face.
I wave goodbye to the point, as it once again sails over
her head and thuds against the
classroom wall.
The clock drags its biggest leg painfully round in
circles. The urge to escape twists my innards.
Like a broken record that thinks it still works, she starts
up again, affecting a tone of voice to
impersonate stupidity, she carries it off effortlessly.
Relishing the giggles from every quarter of the class,
she sings out her patronising pitch of lies
and lines, numbers and numbskulls, angles and
arrogance.
I'm blocking her out. Each pointless word that passes by
is sawn in half and scrapped, like crispy
shavings tumbling from the barrel of a pencil sharpener.
She's as cold and stiff as her numbers; a pious
Pythagoras, a tyrant of trigonometry.

Blue

Deep walls sink into a carpeted shoreline.
The cavernous depths of this room make my heart sprint.
I feel myself inside my body and stomach plummets.
Liberty curtailed and instructed to wait.
Time used like a waterboard.
Only here could the truth deliver such retribution.

Meltdown Haiku #1

Rage boils my blood dry.
Mind blank, sparks misfire
Words disappear.

"Me, Mum & Dolly"

Early lessons in human relations had taught me that I was far from a natural when it came to engaging with other human beings, and especially other children. My struggle in connecting with other kids didn't come from a desire not to, but almost the opposite. My desperate desire to fit in, to be involved and to feel included was painfully obvious — so obvious that even at a young age, I had noticed it. Self-awareness is something I have always been grateful to possess, but from the perspective of a boy just trying to appear normal, it was yet another chapter in a book filled with stresses and anxieties. Having the loud and obnoxious voice of self-awareness in the back of your head whilst trying to juggle facial expressions, talking at the right time, perfecting body language, maintaining the right spatial awareness and attempting to read hundreds of indistinguishable social cues every minute was utterly exhausting. The feeling of being different had always been there, ignored and irrelevant whenever playing alone or at home with my family, but suddenly glaringly obvious and illuminated whenever socialising with others. For many years I struggled to work out what was more exhausting; being weird or pretending not to be; either way I knew it was not normal.

Amidst the early awakenings of self-analysis there was

one person I could rely on. Mum was a single parent; I knew that because a rude boy at school, called Thomas, told me his delightful dad said it meant she was a 'slapper'. When I told mum this, I was surprised that she laughed; people laughing at things that aren't funny has never made sense to me. For me, it was horrifying to hear my own mother called such a thing. Having assessed the word briefly I came to the conclusion it meant she slapped people. Could it be true? Is that what she did when I went to school, or to granda's house? Surely not, you'd have to be horrible to do that and of one thing I was certain; my mum was not horrible. Her laughing only reinforced my growing doubt and concern so I challenged her. "Why are you laughing. It's a terrible thing."

Seeing the seriousness of my furrowed brow she stopped to reassure me; "I haven't been slapping anyone, but I might slap Thomas' dad next time I see him." As she walked away to scrape the remnants of a pasta bake into the bin, she said to herself; "That's rich, coming from a man who screwed his wife's sister." The next time Thomas called me a name, I would be ready, locked and loaded.

My opportunity came a few weeks later when Thomas decided to follow me around at lunch time and accuse me of watching baby programmes on TV. This of course was a complete fabrication, I was eight years old and thoroughly enjoyed the odd episode of Fireman Sam, but what eight-year-old boy didn't? It was hardly as if Thomas, who I thought to myself had the intellect of a neanderthal, was spending his evenings reading the *Financial Times*. I began the process of dealing with

Thomas, as I had been told to do. I walked calmly (we must not run inside) to the receptionist desk and asked for Miss Holly, who often helped to calm me down. We had a formal arrangement, Miss Holly and I, that if anyone such as Thomas was bothering me, rather than reacting I should come and tell her or another teacher. Thomas lurked at the bottom of one of the corridors, like a bad smell, as the receptionist told me that Miss Holly was not in today, I asked for another teacher; "Anyone will do," I told her sternly. I pretended not to notice Thomas as I waited. Moments later a bearded man with a pot belly emerged from the staff room door smelling of coffee and wearing a tracksuit with a stopwatch around his neck, I had not seen him before, but I did not like him already.

"Yes?" he said to me, as I gathered my thoughts and tried to remain calm, "What do you want?" I had no sooner begun my prepared speech when he cut me off;

"You're fighting with someone?"

"No, he's following me around and Miss Holly said if it happened again, I should stay calm and come and…" he interrupted me with a sigh which blew over my face like a coffee-scented cloud;

"Go and find your friends and play some games, lunch will be over soon." And with that, he was gone, the door had literally and figuratively been shut in my face. My thoughts moved onto Thomas who was grinning like a bad guy in a Disney movie at the bottom of the corridor. I took a deep breath and walked toward him, back outside into the playground. Thomas' taunt was no longer about Fireman Sam, it was now a ludicrous accusation that I was a snitch that as he put it 'not even the teachers want to talk to'. This cut deep as in the three times I had employed this technique of involving Miss Holly so far I had felt slightly like I was interfering with her lunch break, but what choice did I have? I was so angry at Thomas that I spun around to face him and seeing this, other kids began to gather round to watch our dispute play out. After a few moments of shouting, it became clear that he was not going to relent, so without thinking, I played my ace. In a moment of perfect silence, I cut across Thomas' jibes about being a lonely little weirdo and said; "YOUR DAD SCREWED HIS WIFE'S SISTER." The backlash was swift. In reality Thomas understood what I had said about as much as I did, but he knew one thing; I had mentioned his dad, and in the hard world of playground law, that was unforgiveable. Whilst I had in the past comforted myself with the belief that Thomas' intelligence was like that of a neanderthal, a caveman, no smarter than Stig of the Dump, I realised too late that he also had the strength and penchant for violence to match. All that nonsense about the pen being mightier than the sword came crashing down around my ears in an unceremonious burst of violence in which I ended up on the ground. I felt the sharp sting of asphalt as I pushed my hands flat and came nose to nose with the playground that was a moment ago beneath by feet.

After regular humiliations like this, it seemed pointless to me to even try interacting with other children, there was clearly a problem and there was one thing I was certain about; that problem lay with me. Many nights after school were spent in tears, hugging my mum and asking her why she didn't make me to be normal, why did I have to be so awkward, so inexplicably me. Her words always reassured me and gave me the courage to keep moving forward. She taught me that even during those darkest school days, I knew that I had a loving home to return to, where we would play mum's country music CD's and dance around the kitchen. What did it matter if other kids thought I was weird? The only people who mattered at home, were me, Mum and Dolly Parton.

Yoghurt Pot Prince

Scissors cut out patient patterns.
I take my place atop turrets in a cardboard castle.
Your hands weave the fabric of my fantasy.
I am crowned the king of daydreams.

What started as a box, you whisper, is now my kingdom.

Long live the recycled regent, the homemade monarch,
the yoghurt pot prince.

Tyrannosaur

"It means king you know. It's the king of all dinosaurs".
I sense the familiar contrast between my enthusiasm and your indifference.
Poor fool I think to myself, now you are wishing you had never asked.
Like a general on the edge of the battle, I observe, through a rusty old looking glass. The delay of distance leaves me to pursue a prickly path where I am eventually ambushed by hindsight.
Roughly seven minutes ago you asked me which is my favourite dinosaur and now the colour continues to leak from your complexion as I hammer more facts into your distracted face.

"They had feathers."
"No, they didn't"
"Yes. They did"
"Not in Jurassic Park"
"Jurassic Park is fake"

As I watch you walk away, the final nail firmly in the coffin lid of conversation, I realise too late my repetitious mistake.
I can creep toward chit chat or cautiously hunt down a conversation and yet before I know it, I awake to find

my foot in my mouth.
An apex predator sabotaged by its own ineptitude, left alone to contemplate its empty stomach and lack of friends.
My day dreams are filled with ancient giants, their names, their habitats and the number of their bones.
I obsess until the cows come home, of diplodocus and brontosaurus. Triceratops lights a flame in my belly that burns for days as I rehearse the names of palaeologists past and present.
Even the adults I know can't remember them all. I unearth knowledge like fossilised bones and realise I may not be normal but neither were they.
The tiny-armed tyrannosaur sits upon a throne of legacy so large, that no one talks about the weakness of his reach.
Not all crowns are made the same and neither are the skulls on which they sit.

Acting Up

I discovered it aged six.
Covering your face in layers of character.
Open dishonestly applauded and awarded.
I'd been doing it for years, like crafting masks and laying bricks

Like a duck to water, I founder my flow
A healthy hobby (with a secret agenda)
Rehearsing words (and conversations)
The script; my guide to interaction
The stage; a playground for deception.

Meltdown Haiku #2

Insides ache and pulse
Tongue too heavy to speak out
Waves of dread crash down

Modern Major General

I am the very model of a modern major general
I can recollect the verses from musicals immemorable.

I have taught myself each line through repetition and through mimicry.

Mr Gilbert and Mr Sullivan were the start of my affinity.
I can speak their words in time and rarely falter with delivery.
Once they're in my brain they will remain until I've done the job
I know librettos book by book from opening to epilogue

It's not a choice that I can make, it soaks in whilst I listen
Of all my fleeting focuses I consider this my mission

So, it may well be a burden to have this brain by chance.
But even when I'm old and grey, I'll sing pirates of Penzance.

Meltdown Haiku #3

Skin fibres vibrate
Sledgehammer thoughts turn to dust
Cuts like broken glass

Love and other processes

You may say, we cannot feel.
You may hear that I feel not.

But I have felt every rockfall from the eruption of anger.
I have felt the solar flames disembowel me with love
and with longing.

I have felt the lonely ice winds of grief lash my bones
and howl into a hurricane within.

My core is made of feeling.

My spine is a book stack of emotions, read back-to-back
and revisited like old friends.

Each jettison of pain and each reassuring glow of
friendship that has grazed, bruised, and healed you, has
touched me too.
But whereas you call out when burnt, my tongue is tied
by binds of my own making.
A towering silence built on foundations of fear. I am its
builder and its prisoner.

Next time when you question if I feel, you should not doubt it.
Because there are those of us who cannot shout about it.

Meltdown Haiku #4

Confused waves circle
Fingers twitch and tongue lies heavy
Inside, the storm grows

Cardboard Socks

I don't make the rules.
Some things are just right.
Like sunlight through stained glass.
Some things are just right.
Like the subdued hum of a summer night.
Some things are just right.
Like soggy Weetabix in your mouth.
I don't make the rules.
Some things are just wrong.
Like cardboard against dry finger tips.
Some things are just wrong.
Like any wet vegetable that crunches.
Some things are just wrong.
Like socks that aren't put on right.
They're wrong if they're not right.
And its right to know what's wrong.
I don't make the rules.

Hour of Madness

I chase my thoughts through the endless caverns of the night and find myself in good company.
Some call it the mad midnight hour and the ghosts we long so much to see play no part in the pantomime.
Those spirits we happily ignore in the daylight, knock on the door and remind us of their presence.
They tread their muddy prints across the threshold into the forefront of our thoughts.
At any moment, you could lose your mind.
It's a short drop and it feels shorter still in this hour when the veil between sanity and madness is thinnest.
Salvation hovers above the horizon line and if you hold fast, you'll see it through. You always do.

Ghost Bird

Shattering the stillness
Sound slaps my skin
Spiked hair stands sharply amid cold sweat
Your cry wakes me as if rocked by dawn or piercing ringtone.
My mind rousing far too late, draws pictures of you holding court over your countryside kingdom.
An effortless acrobat balanced on telephone wires.
A gliding wraith, silent as snowfall, hunting through deep nocturnal fields.
The spectre that rides the twilight until daybreak and greets the light with familiar disdain.
As I return to interrupted dreams, I wish you happy haunting.
Fall into flight, proud guardian of night.

Meltdown Haiku #5

Exhaustion slows thoughts.
A clearer mind feels shameful.
Sleep creeps in with guilt

Tomorrow's Change

With the best laid plans
You can have the worst made days.
Time is dragged by change.

Confronted

Turn around to face.
Dread, like an open casket
Crushed by grief, move on.

Ode to the Poem

To those who gave you hope
To those who dried your tears
To those who raised your spirits
In the hardest, darkest years

To those who stood steadfast
Inspirational to all
To those who set the world aflame
And to those who stopped its fall

To the good, the bad, the ugly
The famous and unknown
To any string of magic words
That calls your soul its home.